THE OAKES PAPERS

Volume 1: May 2015

Examinations of; Inter-religious Communications, Religiosity, Discussion on a two state solution

Contents

Introduction

Welcome to the Oakes Papers, a quarterly forum for the examination of various subjects. Although we will be mainly dealing with international, regional and cultural issues, we will be deviating from these on a regular basis. I created this forum to encourage discussion, debate and hopefully higher learning. Therefore, I am strongly encouraging anyone who may disagree with my conclusions, or wish to contribute to them, to respond in any type of format available to you.

I have also attempted to offer clear and current research information throughout my research process, so if there are any glaring, or not so glaring mistakes, please feel free to let us know. Having clear and concise information to present to our readers is our passion, thus having engaged readership is essential to ensuring that level of quality.

In this first issue, we will be covering topics which were previously presented in academic institutions. The information for these is clearly listed on the cover page of each section. Also our contact information is clearly listed at the end of each volume.

I hope that you enjoy the examinations and are encouraged to respond. I look forward to engaging in meaningful dialogue with all of you. If you would like to become a contributing author, please send a query letter with attached examples to the e-mail address listed at the end of the volume. Thank you for reading and enjoy.

Sincerely,

Rev. Dr. Corey T. Oakes Min.

Author

Esoteric Interfaith Church, Inc.

Interfaith Theological Seminary

Thesis: Natural Law as a basis for Inter-religious communications

Reverend Corey T. Oakes

01 October 2011

Prologue: Here I attempt to explore a line of questioning, which will lead us to some conclusions that I have come to in my research. To begin with we will examine the questions one by, one so as not to stray from our focus. I will begin by posing the major question, and continue with a series of lesser questions. I will then set about answering them in order. I know that this form of structure is unorthodox; however, it is the only way that I have been able to properly convey my ideas, and conclusions. Each major question will act as a complete section, in which we will discuss as many different sides of an argument available. I will also be using some excerpts from other authors, to try to help show the development of the idea.

I will also be using information which has been obtained orally, therefore whenever necessary I will provide information regarding, where to find said information, or similar information in writing.

Outline for Thesis on Natural Law

Introduction:

Natural law has many uses, as well as many versions. The versions that we will be discussing were first used in Ancient Greece. A group called the Stoics, who were so named for the porch of the Agora in Athens, where they lectured and spoke. These Stoics viewed philosophy not as an intellectual past time, but more as a way of life. This led them to a two-fold view in that they believed that it was within man's power to avoid error. They also believed that there was an impression that would come to us in our "revealed reality". This impression could also differ from our learned views. This was the view they used to come up with the Natural law, or a law which is un-changing and occurs throughout the universe. This basic version said that there is a law in nature, which we can all see a certain order, for which we are witness. Aristotle also gives us a version in his Nichomean Ethics, in book 1, he explains that,

"…Every art and every inquiry, and similarly every action and pursuit, is thought to aim at some good; and for this reason the good has rightly been declared to be that at which all things aim.

But a certain difference is found among ends; some are activities, others are products apart from the activities that produce them".—Aristotle.

Aristotle goes into his version farther in his Nichomean Ethics, but for our purposes we will be examining another philosopher, St. Thomas Aquinas, as well as other philosophers. Specifically, we will be discussing Aquinas's Summa Theologica I and II. In his Summa Theologica II; The Treatise on Law, Part 1 of Second Part Q. 90. Art. 4(Questions XC-Question C). In response to the question, Whether Law is something pertaining to reason? He replies with a Reply Objection (2, pg. 206, Paragraph 1.). Where he states; "Just as in external action we may consider the work, and the work to be done, for instance the work of building, and the house built, so in the acts of reason, we may consider the act itself of reason, that is, to understand and to reason, and something produced by this act." In this he is demonstrating the difference of inward action, and the outcome of said action. This is a very poignant point, especially when considering Natural Laws, as most are based in the ability to generally reason. In order for us to better understand what St. Thomas is trying to say here, I think that we must first look at what he was attempting to achieve overall, with his Summa Theologica.

First, I believe that he was attempting to answer most of the fundamental questions of his day, especially the legitimacy of the churches laws, and dogma. In doing so he was in fact able to answer more than just the questions concerning religious views of his time, but was also able to answer some of the age old philosophical questions as well. Consider that the most influential powers of his day were the church, and king, and both were heavily addressed in his work. However, this in fact laid the ground work for a lot of the great thinkers to come later, such as Thomas Hobbes, and many of the enlightenment thinkers, giving them the basis for arguments against the king's powers, as well as gave them a foundation with which to base the rights of the common man as well. This brings us to my next version for which I would like to examine, that of Thomas Hobbes, and his views on how this law should be treated.

Hobbes viewed Natural Law, as the only true basis for actual laws, (otherwise known as Positive Laws), he is quoted as saying, "A law that is not just, is no law at all". In this very popular phrase he is explaining the way in which the Natural Laws, or "laws of reason, and virtue", are used to check the positive laws of a state or nation.

I will also be using information that I have collected from various Native American teachers, as well as some of the other great philosophers, and modern thinkers, such as Grotius, Carmichael, Campbell, and possibly some Pufendorf. Prior to, or immediately following each of my references to them, I will ensure that I include a way to access the information given.

If there are any concerns or questions please feel free to contact me either by e-mail, or through the Northernway Seminary.

Thesis on Natural Law, and the Divine Laws

Thesis Statement:

The questions, which I will be exploring, are a series of questions designed to be added to, or explored further by the readers. As this is the goal, they are meant to cause some debate, and discussion. As previously stated, I will be focusing on the religious aspects of Natural Law, but will be touching on some of the political and legal aspects slightly, as they will inevitably have some overlap to their understandings.

What is Natural Law? Well it is the Law of Nature, or a theory which posits the existence of a law whose content is set by nature and that therefore has validity everywhere. It is also sometimes opposed to the "Positive law", or the laws of the state, and can therefore be used as a standard by which to criticize that law. Used in this way however, natural law can be used more to criticize the statute, and not so much for the actual law itself. There are also many different versions of Natural law such as, those used to determine the role that morality plays in determining legal and societal norms. There are also a great number of legal and political theorists, who have used Natural Law, to determine what Natural Rights the "common" man has in the political systems of both Europe as well as the United States. However we will be dealing with the different interpretations, having to do with the common goods, morality, as well as divinity. As these are all tools to help develop good Interfaith Discussions.

As previously stated, I will begin by asking a "major question", and then proceed to the "sub-questions". I will attempt to do this in a manner which is easy to follow, so as to get my ideas across properly.

We then will proceed to question, 1. (A.) Is Natural Law a Divine Law, or is it a common understanding, which can lead us to the Divine Laws? I answer that, No Natural Law is not a Divine law; however, in some cultures, such as Native Americans, or Aborigine tribes of Australia, there can be some uses of Natural law, as a form of Divine law, as there is some correlation between their customs, and their general understandings of a Natural Law, or "Divine Nature"; thereby giving a sense of a "Divine Natural Law". Aside from these "Natural Cultures", divine law must be devoutly separated from the "common Natural Law"; unless divine intervention is a pre-condition.

As for the basis for which to find a Divine law; I answer yes, as it is a pre-cognition to know, or to "understand", some form of early Natural Laws. "Now those things are said to be self-evident to us the knowledge of which is naturally implanted in us, as we can see in regard to the first principals".-St. Thomas Aquinas.(Summa Theologica 1.Q2-A1., Obj.1.). Here he explains the self-evident nature of Gods existence. It is my belief that this also proves knowledge of the "Natural Order "or, innate knowledge of omnipotent presence. In other words, the knowledge which we are born with, that tells us that there is something larger than ourselves. To some this may simply be the family unit to which they are born. To others this may mean the culture or set of similar beliefs to which they are born. Still to others, it is the proof of god's existence, as well as proof he is within us .I believe that it is proof that, we are born with the ability to learn, and become a part of our world, as well as our place in it. Many have viewed this as the proof of order to the universe, and of cycles within that universe. This proof of cycles, can lead us to a "common sense", or otherwise known as a common understanding of the universe in which we live (Reid). This leads me to my next line of questioning, which is; if we are to use natural law as a common understanding, then we must ask, what is the common understanding?, and how can we use this understanding to find the good in human nature, i.e., the "Divine". I answer that as far as we can ascertain, the "common" in common understanding, is largely a misconception, as most of the general populace has no "true" understanding of the Natural laws, as we have defined them, aside from the occasional use of some general terminology acquired during general interactions. Therefore we must first examine some of the versions of "Divine" Laws, as well as how the different views came to be, or as they were understood in their time. We will begin by examining St. Thomas Aquinas, a 15th century Philosopher, and Monk.

Divine Law as set by, St. Thomas Aquinas; asserts, that, Natural law, as the perfection of human reason, could approach but not fully comprehend the Eternal Law, so therefore should be supplemented by Divine Law. The Eternal Law, which he explains in this quote is; "a law is nothing else but a dictate of practical reason emanating from the ruler who governs a perfect community. That the whole community of the universe is governed by Divine Reason".—St. Thomas Aquinas (Summa Theologica II, Question XCI, Article 1.). Although, St. Thomas Aquinas believed that all things were handed down by God, he also believed that man could use right reason, and that by doing so, would become closer to what God had intended us to be. We will examine more of St. Thomas, later, for now we will examine Hugo Grotius, a Swedish philosopher, as well as a political Theorist, who lived during the 16th century. He was the prodigy son of a curator of the University of Leyden, who started at that same university at the age of eleven. He is often considered to be the father of international law.

Divine Law as set by, Hugo Grotius; "Natural law is the Dictate of Right Reason, indicating that any act... is forbidden, or commanded by God... the Author of Nature...Natural law is so immutable that it cannot be changed by God himself. Divine Laws (which are eternal) are created directly by God."(De iure belli ac pacis, Prolegomeni XI).Here, we see that Grotius separates the natural from the divine. He does this so as to show the differences, between man's abilities, and those which are handed down by the divine. He sees Natural Law as man's innate ability to reason for himself, without the need for intervention from the divine. He does not however, say that there is no duty to the divine laws, just because there is an innate ability, on the contrary, he sees it more as, bestowed upon us at birth by the creator, and therefore our responsibility to use properly, or for just means. This responsibility, as he envisioned it, should be used to help create a more just, and equal society. This leads us back to Aristotle, often called the father of Natural Law. Divine Law as Aristotle saw it is not exactly Divine Law, it is more of a view on the natural states, as well a sort of inner forum that takes place. For instance;

"…in the continent man it obeys the rational principal, and presumably in the temperate and brave man it is still more obedient; for in him it speaks, on all matters, with the same voice as the rational principle.(The Works of Aristotle II; *Nicomachean Ethics*, Book I; 25.).

Here we come to, the common, in common understanding. Aristotle sees the divine law as a means to which we are driven to do good and rational things. He sees man as having the ability to be rational, and kind, yet only when we listen to our inner voice, or conscience. I believe that this is the understanding, which most people have. The innate knowledge then would be our ability to reason, as well as our ability to understand our environment and our place within it. Also, that if we listen to that inner voice, we are essentially using Natural Law, or "Right Reason". This is sometimes also referred to as, "common sense", but what is common sense? The term common sense is thought to also refer to an innate knowledge which we all share. It was examined by a group of Scottish Theorists in the eighteenth century, and was called, "the common sense theory". One of these theorists was Gershom Carmichael a professor of Moral philosophy at Glasgow University. He was also a conduit into Scotland of the European Natural law tradition. A tradition of scientific investigation of human nature with a view to constructing an account of the principles that are morally binding on us. In his work entitled; Natural Rights, he writes;

" Due cultivation of the mind involves filling it with sound opinion regarding our duty, learning to judge well the objects which commonly stimulate our desires and acquiring rational control of our passions.(Natural Rights, p. 48-49).

Carmichael was good at deconstructing the philosophical viewpoints, so as to put them into terms that could be easily explained. I mention him because, to see common sense through the eyes of Carmichael, helps us to develop a more well defined idea of what that common sense is. Another view point is that of Campbell, who believed that;

"…common sense is an original source of knowledge common to humankind, by which we are assured of a number of truths that cannot be evinced by reason, and it is equally impossible, without a full conviction of them, to advance a single step in the acquisition of knowledge" (Philosophy of Rhetoric, vol. 1, p. 114).

This particular view is one that I believe; best describes common sense, as we know it today. This is that there is an order to the universe, which gives us a basis by which to judge our actions, laws, and rhetoric. Giving us also the basis for further judging our rights, and responsibilities to ourselves, and our communities. Therefore, the common knowledge which we share seems to be based on shared common truths, on which we all agree. These theories give us a position from which to easier judge the following line of inquiry. Therefore, I would like to return somewhat to my earlier focus of study, starting with my next question. Q.2B. Are the Divine Laws applicable as a basis for inter-religious discussions on; "Amicable Ability"? Amicable Ability, being the ability to reside or, take some action, only amicably, or with regards to all parties involved. For example; If you were to own a piece of land, and a tree from your neighbor's house is growing into your basement. The neighbor and you decide to take action before it gets into your basement. This is amicable ability, or the ability to act, with regard to the other involved parties. Therefore the question becomes, can we act amicably in the actions we take, when they involve other parties, now that we have an idea of what amicable ability is.

I answer; yes, by imploring to their respected religious bases, we may in fact be able to act, in regards to our neighbors. Although, many religious groups do not agree, they do all have various similarities, in their teachings. These various teachings give us the ability, to find a common ground. I believe that common ground to be Natural Law, as it is the most prevalent idea found in more than one religious interpretation. This also gives us the common reasoning with which to further develop a discussion based on common understanding instead of basing a discussion on regional or cultural differences.

The Catholic religion has a version; based mainly on the writings of St. Thomas Aquinas, as well as the writings of St. Augustine, and St. Benedict. The Muslim religion has a version, which is based mostly on the writings of Abu-Mansur of the Maturidi School of Sunni Theology.

There are many versions, in many religions, as well as in, Politics, Law, and International Law. Even the United States constitution, is partly based in Natural law …life, liberty, and the pursuit of happiness… (U.S.Constitution). Therefore, if all of the religions have some form of understanding, of natural law, then is it not the common ground we seek? Let us examine then, the proper uses of Natural Law in regards to the inter-religious conversations. In analyzing the proper uses, you should first look to the classical interpretations, with regards to a more modern viewpoint. First, let us look at a version of the classical Greek natural law, presented by Paul Foriers and Chaim Perelman in the History of ideas. In their paper they describe it as;

"The idea of natural law is tied to the conception of an organized universe; the idea can be disengaged only after a society has become aware of the regularity, the succession, the repetition of natural phenomenon, the existence of cycles and the ability to make predictions, predictability based on the existence of inter-relations with the physical world (Perelman 2).

The reason I use this version is to show how the classical view can be re-examined using a modern eye so to speak. By doing so we find that it can be used to see the inter-relationship between the major religions of the world. It also shows the viewpoint of a world view, and not just a regional type of viewpoint. So, in essence there should be some form of re-examination that occurs, prior to the discussion. In this way, you can easier examine, both your side of the discussion, as well as identify key points to consider, on the other side. Consider, their faith, as much as you consider your own. In this way, you will be able to construct a discussion, based in commonalities, instead of differences. For instance; if you were to attempt a discussion between say, the Irish Catholic population of Northern Ireland, and the Protestant population, you should consider their respective histories, as well as common problems. This helps when trying to find some common ground, as both of these parties have a lot of common ground in their respective histories. Also, there are a lot of common socioeconomic issues, such as health, safety, and of course economic. These issues at best only offer a simple starting point, however a starting point which is built on commonality, will hold better than one built on differences. So what are these different interpretations?

I will begin by examining the Muslim tradition, as it is shorter than the others. In the Maturidi School of Sunni Theology, they have come to posit the existence of a form of Natural law. Based on the writings of Abu Mansur al-Maturidi who stated that the human mind could know of the existence of God and the major forms of "good and evil", without the help of revelation. Also, there is the concept of *Istslah* in Islamic Law. Which states that the "good" in "common good" is whatever is connected to one of the basic five goods; religion, life, lineage, property, and reason (The Maturidi School of Sunni Theology, the writings of Abu Mansur al-Maturidi). These five basic goods are extremely similar to the fundamental beliefs of the western world, giving us a good starting point for discussion. They also, very much resemble the contractualism of Thomas Hobbes, who was one of the most prolific of the western philosophers. It also bears a lot of resemblance to the theories of St. Thomas Aquinas, as well as those of Aristotle.

Therefore, using these similar understandings, can give us similar grounds for an inter-faith discussion. Given the similarities between these, seemingly different religions, in regards to these understandings, can there also be other correlations? Of course there are, there are even legal similarities, as well as usage similarities, which we will explore at another time.

Another version which I would like to discuss is the Contemporary Christian version. Although there are many different interpretations of this version, we will be concerning ourselves with Thomas Hobbes and his Leviathan. In chapter XIV, entitled "of the first and second laws; and of contracts", he explains that which he finds these laws to be, and I agree. According to Hobbes; the first law of nature is "that every man ought to endeavor peace, as far as he has hope of obtaining it; and when he cannot obtain it, that he may seek and use all helps and advantages of war". The second law of nature is "that a man be willing, when others are so too, as far forth, as for peace, and defense of himself he shall think it necessary, to lay down this right to all things; and be contented with so much liberty against other men, as he would allow other men against himself". He goes on to other laws, nineteen in all; however we will resign ourselves to these. First let us discuss the first natural law, according to Hobbes. The former law is one of the base principals for which I am basing my discussion upon, as it deals with the laws which govern nations, and theocracies. These areas are where most of our interfaith discussions will occur. Therefore, we will examine them with this in mind. The basics of this law are to be understood, not as a means by which to justify war, but a reason to stay at the "table". It is my own understanding that; we should endeavor to peace, long before we endeavor to war, (which is our current case). If we are to use it in this way, we must always consider it as a beginning, due to its ability to be misinterpreted, and therefore used as a means to change the tone in the discussions.

What I believe Hobbes is telling us is that if we are diligent in our understandings of our own position, then we should be just as well informed upon our opposition's position as well. Thereby we will all be better equipped to endeavor for peace. Thus, leading us to the second natural law according to Hobbes. This is of course;

"…that a man be willing, when others are so too, as far forth as for peace and defense of himself he shall think it necessary to lay down this right to all things, and be contented with so much liberty against other men, as he would allow other men against himself"(Hobbes XIV).

This law is crucial as it discusses not only our reciprocal duties, but the reciprocal duties to others. In other words it is our duty to be willing to give up some parts of our position, in order that they will also be willing to give parts of their position. This creates an environment of cooperation, and not an environment of competition. However Hobbes does remind us not to give more than we receive. In this way we are attempting to create an even position between all involved parties. Having no more standing than the other parties, can also help those parties who feel the most threatened to feel more equal to the rest of the parties involved.

Although Hobbes is not the most common version of the Christian faith, he is in my opinion the best one to look at in the cases of contracts, which is what an interfaith discussion is. However, I would like to show a small piece of another contemporary Christian version, the Catholic understanding. The Catholic Church understands human beings to consist of, body and mind, or the physical and non-physical. Also those human beings are capable of discerning good and evil, due to their conscience. They further rely on St. Thomas Aquinas, to explain the remainder of their position. However, we do find a lot of correlations between the Hobbesian theories, and those of Aquinas. Generally, it is their belief that the natural laws guide us through divine providence, and that understandings of it are developed through rigorous devotion. I show these, to show that even though there are different theories, for different religions, they are generally very similar. Therefore, we can easily use these similarities to our advantage, when attempting to construct a viable and equitable discussion.

This leads us to my next line of questioning, which is; are we resigned to using these classical interpretations? I answer that; no, although we can use these classical interpretations to help us to better understand our modern position, yet they should be somewhat resigned to this. I believe that there is much we can learn from these interpretations, but they are only a base of understanding with which to better judge the world in which we live today. Therefore, we must ask; can we re-examine them for a more modern view? I most emphatically answer, yes, as I think that we must re-examine them as there are more factors to consider in this modern world, than these interpretations offer in there classical form. This must be our first step in achieving a new understanding for the modern use. Let us examine why.

First there is the problem of the time period in which most of these theories were postulated. In their time, these were the most advanced ideas of equality and freedom, in the world, due to the status-quo, which was that most countries were governed by either a monarchy, or a theocracy. Given the fact that these systems offered little, or no freedom to the common man, they offered much to the people of the time. However in our modern world, there is a lot more consideration given to the freedoms of the masses, and therefore we have less need of acquiring our freedoms through theories of how to be governed, and more to gain through re-examination of those freedoms, in order to come to a more equitable understanding of them, and how they are applied. This gives us the ability to use these earlier versions, to postulate newer versions which will be more applicable to our current state. By doing so, we may be able to come to a more equitable understanding between the various religious entities. This leads me now to positive law, or the laws of man. These are the laws in which we have entrusted our governing parties to make in order that we may live in relative safety, and security. As these are the laws that generally guide most men, they too must be re-examined to understand the differences in the respective societies, and how that will correlate to interfaith discussions.

As previously stated, these laws can be judged according to natural law, thereby giving them the ability to better mold these laws in to more equitable uses, giving thought as to how they will be used in the deconstructed humanitarian sense. Doing this will ensure a more inclusive and equitable discussion, giving all parties involved, a more even position. It will also ensure that you know the ways in which the other parties will view these laws. For if we are to have any kind of a discussion with a viable outcome, then we must always consider the society, as well as the culture in which we are trying to engage in a discussion as they will invariably view these things differently than you.

The positive laws that we are discussing are generally concerning the humanitarian aspect of a given society, however they may also concern, how that society views dealings with others outside of that society, and so must be examined in some detail prior to beginning any form of discussion with them.

In Summary, if we are to have any kind of an amicable discussion between religious entities, we must prepare ourselves, as well as our positions prior to any kind of discussion, so as to consider all of the aspects of entering into that discussion. As we have discussed, there are many different forms of natural law, and just as many different uses of these versions, however most of these versions also offer a common basis for discussions. Therefore it is my understanding that if we use these different versions to our advantage, we will find that they can give us a basis for which to find common goals, as well as common understanding, In the world in which we live today. Common understanding is difficult to come by, but by striving to find that common understanding, we will invariably find some degree of common ground. If we can somehow find this common ground, then we can find hope that we will be able to better solve our differences, without always resorting to violent means to get our views expressed.

In the case of the Christian and Muslim issues, these laws can have a profound effect on the discussions, in regards to the different levels of freedoms that each side wishes to have. Although there is obviously much more to consider in their case, I do believe that by pursuing this avenue of commonalities, we can solve the differences in their respective positions, so far as their respective economic, geographic and humanitarian positions. In fact the use of natural law in this particular discussion should be the only basis for their interfaith discussion, as these two religious entities have centered on their differences for thousands of years, and have become extremely polarized as a result.

Therefore using natural law seems to be the only way to get them to agree on at least one position, as both versions offer a similar understanding. This would give a position with which to amicably agree on some individual terms, even if they will not budge on their positions overall. Therefore, I find that if you can use natural law as they understand it, you can then correlate it to the other positions own understanding, thereby giving you some common ground, with which to discuss the differing positions. Although I have not gone into great detail about which natural laws to use, or not use, I do believe that I have presented an idea of what natural law is, as well as some of it uses in an interfaith discussion. I will then conclude by saying that; if we are to coexist as human beings on a planet that we all must share, then we must find a way to discuss our differences, and not just destroy each other based on those differences.

If there are any questions regarding this paper, or Natural Law, then please feel free to ask:

Rev. Dr. Corey T. Oakes, Minister of Natural Law

1013 Apt. C 5th Street

Wenatchee, Washington

98801

Or: corey-oakes@hotmail.com

A general survey of religiosity levels of Americans is a determining factor in their positions regarding the two-state solution of the Palestinian State, and the Israeli State.

Corey Oakes

Whatcom Community College

April 2012

Table of Contents

Introduction

    There have been many studies done concerning the two-
state solution, which is one of the proposed solutions to the Gaza
Strip situation in the Middle East (Springborg 2008:166-170). The
basics of this proposed solution are that Palestine becomes their
own country, and Israel remains, giving both the powers of
National Statehood, each with their own separate economy,
education, and governance. Historically this has been a solution
proposed by many scholars on both sides of the issue, but mostly
by groups associated with the United States, Israel, the PLO,
Fatah and similar Palestinian groups (Abbas 2012).

    Many of these studies have looked at various elements in
regards to these two groups, and their situation (Reuveny 1999).
Some of which have dealt with the economies, and their relative
interdependence (Springborg 2008). Others have looked at the
religious preferences of those who live in the areas of both the
West Bank, as well as Gaza, using data collected during polling
over a seven year period (Tessler and Nachtwey 1999).

    We will be looking at how the religious attitude of a small
number of Americans affects their viewpoint on the two-state
solution. It is my belief, that there will be some correlation
between the religious attitudes of some religions, and their

position in regards to the two-state solution. Some of these religions have even released into the national media, their official positions concerning the Israeli-Palestinian Conflict (CBN 2013). However, they do not represent the entire religions as a whole, and do not provide us with any actual data, just opinion, and official position of one particular group.

Review of Literature

Of the studies available, few support the idea that the religiosity level of individuals affects their position on the two-state solution (Tessler and Nachtwey 1999). In fact most studies suggest quite the opposite that the religiosity of individuals has little to no effect on their position, in regards to the two-state solution. In the study performed by Mark Tessler and Jodi Nachtwey, they examined data from surveys performed by the Center for Palestinian Studies and research (CPRS) in Nablus, in the West Bank (Tessler and Nachtwey 1999). The questions were geared toward examining the support for a two-state solution among those living in the West Bank, over the age of eighteen. Of those surveyed the support for groups who were historically opposed to a peace accord with Israel had dropped, and been replaced with a null support, or lack of overall confidence in any group, as stated in their report entitled; Palestinian Political

Attitudes: An Analysis of Survey Data from the West Bank and Gaza;

> "Rather, it appears that some supporters of Islamic and Leftist movements and of Nationalist Independents, in all three cases, decided that they were not satisfied with any faction, and they accordingly gave their endorsements to 'none of the above'"(Tessler and Nachtwey 1999:2).

This however is only representative of those studied, who live in the West Bank and Gaza, and says nothing of the attitudes experienced by Americans in Washington State.

One other study performed by Robert Springborg looks at the differences between the religious Islam, and the political Islam (2008). Although the study looks at Islam in Turkey and Indonesia, it is also applicable here, as it reflects attitudes of Islamic individuals, and their political attitudes. In his report to the Middle East Policy Council in spring of 2008, Springborg states;

> "While the politically and economically benign environments of Turkey and Indonesia underlay the emergence of moderate, development-focused Islamism there, in Palestine and Lebanon the shortcomings of state and nation are reflected in the radical,

violence prone nature of Hamas and Hezbollah"(Springborg 2008:166-170).

Many of the conclusions in these studies, leads us to the economic situation between Israel and Palestine. A study by Rafael Reuveny looks at this element and its effects on the overall relations between the two groups;

"My focus is on the economic and political problems of the current Israeli-Palestinian economic interdependence, analyzing the experience of the 1990s as an integrated natural experiment" (Reuveny 1999).

This is one of the correlates we were looking at in the survey, to see if there was any correlation between the income levels, and the opinions expressed in regard to the occupation variable. In the study he discusses some of his conclusions, one of which is;

"….that a Palestine that is economically autonomous may well be a better Israeli neighbor than a Palestine that is economically dependent on Israel"(Reuveny 1999:668).

These examinations, as well as others, help us to understand the various elements involved in the studies of the situation between Israel and Palestine. One of the most compelling examples of a showcase of elements would be the letter from the Palestinian President to the Israeli Prime Minister. In this letter he states a great many political points; however he also states a good deal of the more complex issues concerning the ongoing relations (Abbas 2012). One of the major issues involved is the occupation of Palestine by Israel in 1967, as illustrated in this excerpt from Palestinian President Abbas's letter;

"Signed agreements, international law, and UN resolutions all recognize that peace will only be realized upon the end of Israel's occupation of Palestinian land that began in 1967. Until such time, Article 7 of the interim agreement stipulated that both parties, Israel and the PLO, shall not take any steps that would prejudice final status negotiations" (Abbas 2012:193).

All of these help to support a position of changing preferences, and attitudes among the populations concerned, but what of the counter elements? First let us look at the results of a Pew Research study. In their study they looked at the views of Americans concerning the Israeli-Palestinian dispute, and how if any they have changed in recent years;

"Regarding the Israeli-Palestinian dispute, far more Americans continue to say they sympathize with Israel rather than

Palestinians (by 48% to 11%). These opinions are little changed in recent years" (Pew Research 2011).

They also examine the relation between political party, and views on the Israeli-Palestinian issues as well as religiosity and views on the same issues;

"There continue to be substantial partisan, ideological and religious differences in views of the Israeli-Palestinian dispute. Fully 75% of conservative Republicans sympathize more with Israel-by far the highest percentage of any partisan group" (Pew Research 2011).

They go on to explain that a majority of "white evangelical Protestants" support the Israeli position as well (Pew Research 2011). Although these results help to support the theory that religiosity does have a significant effect on Americans views regarding the Israeli-Palestinian Conflict, they are not all together conclusive, as they only sampled a population of 1,509 adults. This does not explain what the parameters of "adult" are, nor does it tell us where or how the sample was surveyed, and therefore we should remain slightly wary of these results.

After some review of these studies, I find that I am inclined to agree more with the results of the earlier tests, especially considering the results of our own survey. The results of the Pew Research Survey, do offer some compelling data concerning the attitudes of Americans towards the Israeli-Palestinian Conflict, but I believe that they are not compelling enough for me to dispute the other studies.

Hypothesis

I hypothesize that the religiosity levels of Americans, is a determining factor in their positions regarding the two-state solution of the Palestinian State, and the Israeli State, as well as education as a determining factor, as opposed to those who are not religious.

Methodology

A survey of ten variables was given to twenty-five individuals in the town of Sedro-Wooley, Washington, outside of the local food pavilion over a two day period of time. I used a simple random method to administer the questionnaire survey, which contained closed ended questions. These questions were designed to be simple, and easy to understand, as many of the expected respondents may not have a working knowledge of the conflict between Palestine and Israel. The first four questions in my survey consisted of demographic variable, considered general in nature. These consist of things such as, gender, age, household yearly income, and education. The remaining six questions are listed below in the number and order as in the survey.

5. Do you consider yourself a democrat, republican, independent, or of course no party preference?

6. Do you consider yourself Christian, Jewish, Buddhist, Muslim, Hindu, or some other religion, or of course not religious?

7. How often do you attend religious or spiritual services in a month?

8. In your opinion, should the Palestinian people have their own country?

9. Do you agree with the Israeli occupation of the West Bank?

10. Do you think that Peace in the Middle East is possible?

I chose these questions because, I believe that they represent the best clustering for the layman to follow, and therefore answer in a more informed fashion. Also, I believe that they helped to frame the questioning in such a way, as to bring about a true representative answer from the respondents questioned.

The results of the survey were interesting in that they were not what I had expected to find. The frequency tables show that the majority of respondents were males at 56%, compared to the females at 44%. They also showed that they were between the ages of 25-34, with 40%, and that their income level was under $10,000, with 32% of the respondents within this range. Of these individuals there was 40% who think that Palestine should have their own country. However, this was also found to be equal to the number of respondents who did not agree that Palestine should have their own country, as shown in the graph labeled Own country.

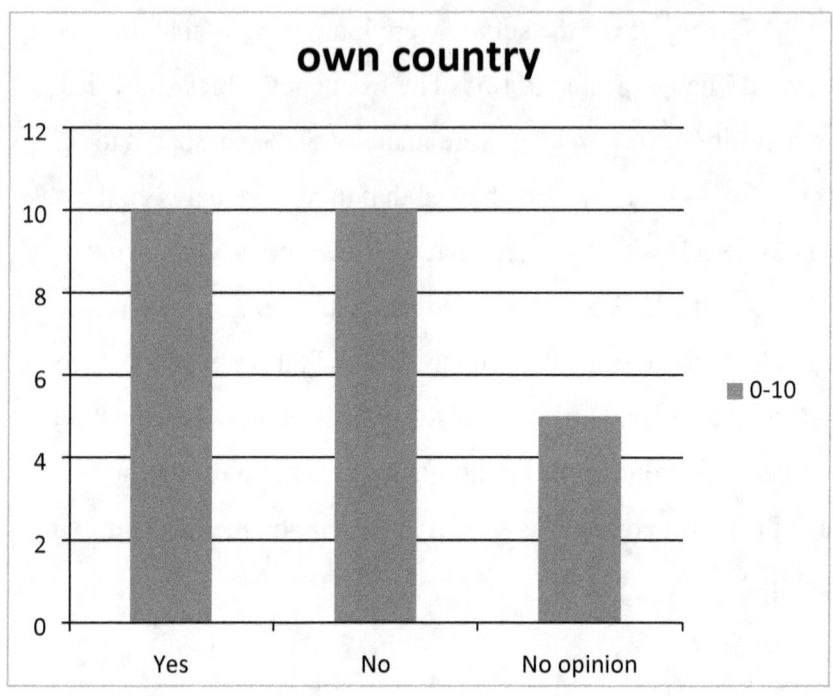

The data also showed that of those surveyed who identified as Christian, the overwhelming majority were not in favor of the Palestinians having their own country, as shown in

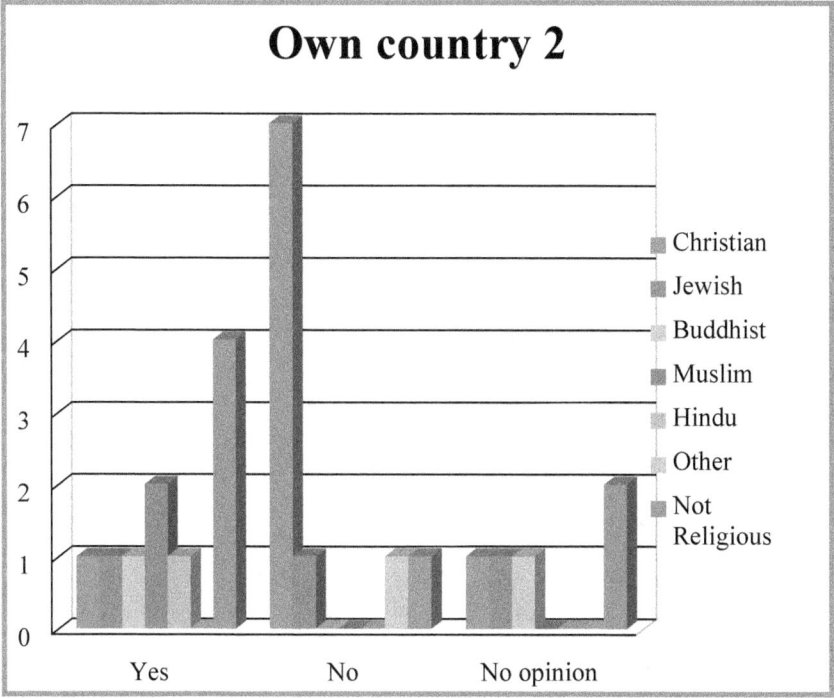

Own country 2

Christian
Jewish
Buddhist
Muslim
Hindu
Other
Not Religious

Yes   No   No opinion

the graph labeled Own country 2. This is consistent with the findings of the Pew Research study that we discussed earlier (Pew Research 2011).

There was also small amount of causation seen amongst the ages of 18-24 year olds, and the belief that peace is possible in the Middle East, as well as some causation with 25-34 year olds, who do not agree that peace in the Middle East is possible.

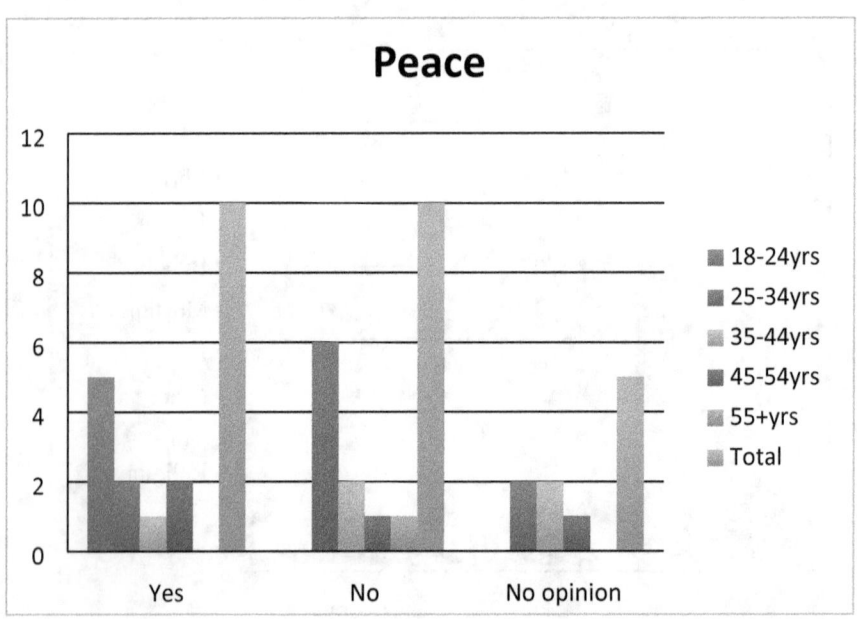

These results may indicate that both age and religious affiliation have some causal relationship with an individual's viewpoint on the Israeli-Palestinian two-state solution. However, the majority of the data collected during the survey would suggest that there is little or no real causal relationship between ones religious affiliation, and their views on the two-state solution.

Conclusion

In conclusion, I find that there is indeed some correlation between Americans from Sedro-Wooley's religious affiliations and their views concerning the Israeli-Palestinian dispute. At least among Christian males between the ages of 25-34 years, who attend religious services once a week. However, the data also showed that there were a lot of no opinion answers, which may indicate that the opinions of those in the survey sample are not representative of individual elements making up Sedro-Wooley, or Skagit County in general.

However, the results of my study are also not consistent with the research studies analyzed for this paper (Springborg 2008). In Springborg's research he found that there really was no real correlation between religious affiliation and their position in regards to the two-state solution. Also we found that there was no data to represent any correlation between educational achievement levels, and the American views on the occupation of Palestine by Israel, as represented in the graph labeled education.

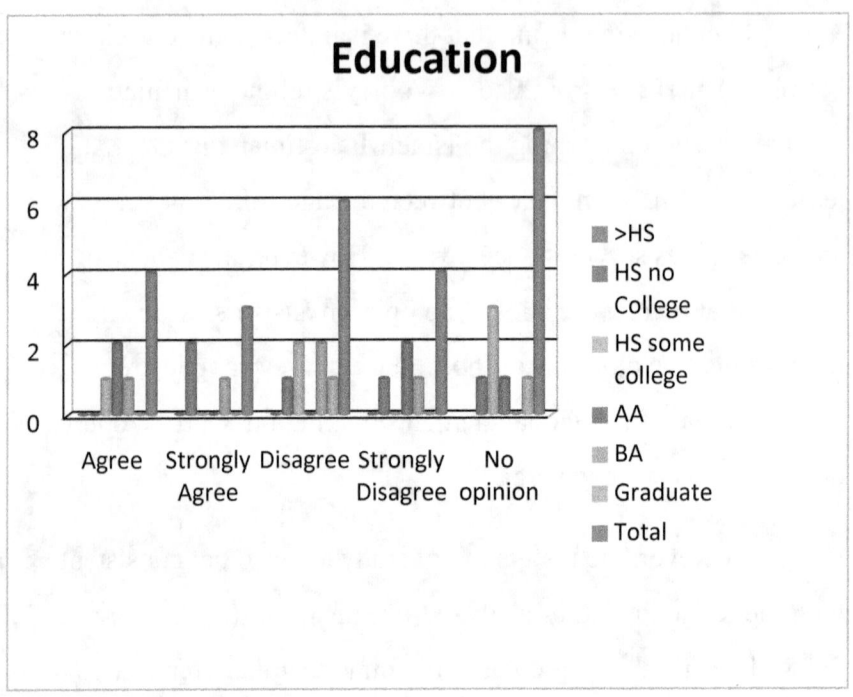

Limitations of Study

There are a great number of limitations concerning this study, such as the limited number of elements in the study. Also the sample size of 25 is an insufficient number for inferring any causal relationships, to the population of Sedro-Wooley as a whole. The study in regards to the two-state solution requires a more stratified interview structure, than the simple random sampling used in this instance. The amount of studies available regarding this subject matter are not up-to-date, and do not include American survey data, as much as those who live in the area, and therefore requires more study in the American arena, before any real conclusions can be drawn. Of those studies which did garner some data which was useful for our purposes, only one of them sought to survey the American population concerning their views on the Israeli-Palestinian dispute (Pew Research 2011), however, that study did not include much of the variable information required for a reasonable analysis of the data, and is therefore of lesser value in regards to this study.

Much more research needs to be done in order to find any real causal relationships between ones individual religiosity, and the views concerning the Israeli-Palestinian Conflict. Those studies must include a larger sample frame, as well as a more representative sample group from which to find respondents. They must also include more variables concerning the religiosity, and attitudes of those respondents selected.

Small Steps In The Holy Land

July 2014

The issues involved in the peace process for the Middle East are varied and complex situations which have been derived from years of argument. Have they really worked in favor of the peace process though, or are they simply unattainable provisions which neither side will agree to, thus leading to a sort of permanent discord? If we are to look seriously at the issues which confront these two parties in the 21st century, then we must really look to issues which can be solved, rather than using the same points in different peace plans. It is my contention that by using smaller more attainable goals which benefit both sides, we can better build a path to actual lasting peace. I will be examining some of the issues which have worked in past agreements, as well as using new examinations of points which are more likely to work given the overall situation in the region since 1967. My examinations will somewhat be general in nature and based on points of agreements and resolutions which were derived from informational sources. They are intended to give a framework for further examinations as a testable hypothesis, not a concise historical representation.

First let us take a minute to examine the past points of agreement in order to help us in our hypothesis. According to the U.S. State Departments information, the 1998 Wye Agreement gave the parties the reciprocity agreement (US State 1998). This reciprocity agreement was meant to deal with issues which they had in common (US State 1998). This reciprocity is the success of the overall recent agreements, as this point gives the parties the ground work for building agreements based on shared issues, even though the later Oslo Agreements were foregone in favor of rising tensions following the death of PLO leader Yasser Arafat (US State 1998). I find that this success is one that can be built upon by using a shared economic reality due to the forces of Globalization and International commerce. My reasoning for this is that due to the blockades imposed upon the Palestinian territories, that economic reciprocity is a viable option for consideration given the shared interests in the region itself. In other words, the current environment in the region lends itself to cooperation through economic reasoning, as both parties would benefit from a heightened economic state. Using this fact in order to affect a ceasefire seems more plausible than using historically non-effective points of contention, or military tactical reasoning, as seems to be the case in previous peace plans (US State 1998).

As this is an examination of using economics as a theoretical path to peace, I would like to move on to the examination of the principles for which this can be possible. In a thesis on inter-religious communications, it was found that using natural law as well as economic and educational concerns, was able to affect cooperative group agreements (Oakes 2011). This helps to show that differing religious organizations can find shared issues on which to base further cooperation amongst their respective regions, albeit on a much smaller group and individual basis. However, these structural similarities show that this approach may have some success in a macro-group environment as well. These points combined with the existing reciprocity agreements, as well as further amendments to these agreements, gives a historical basis for further examination of the economic paths which have reciprocal benefits to the parties involved.

So what are the economic considerations in the region? According to Robert Cherry who conducted an examination of Arab peoples living in Israel, the gap in per capita income has an effect on the levels of conflict between the respective groups (Cherry 2014). This helps to show that the levels of economic stability within the Arab community within Israel, which relate to conflict, are likely transferrable to the larger Arab community outside of Israeli borders, namely the Palestinian community of peoples. If these considerations are then applied to the situation in Palestine, it could be argued that the levels of animosity and conflict would likely lower, due to the lessening of the gap between the median incomes of both parties involved. Achieving this level of economic stability however, requires certain specific areas of international consideration, such as international trade and commerce, as well as stimuli which compels the parties to attempt the economic cooperation, instead of previous security concerns.

If the considerations of international trade and commerce are applied to mutually beneficial areas of the respective groups GDP, then the argument for cooperative economic stability in the region takes on more merit, as it then becomes a question of whether or not the activities in the region will disrupt the trade and commerce of the mutually beneficial areas. This has the potential to lead to more mutually beneficial policy agreements between the parties involved, as both parties would then have more to gain by cooperation, than by conflict.

This can be achieved through creating the economic stimuli of cooperative business practices in the region, combining interests from both parties in one trade or business. This then lessens the need for blockading of ports and avenues to commerce by the occupying state, as well as lessening the incentive for the opposing group's radicalization, by offering economic avenues to their freedoms rather than constant conflict. By creating businesses that use existing resources such as mutual products and services provided by both parties individually, combined into one cooperative structure, both parties achieve higher levels of international and domestic economic stability. This combined with building these cooperative businesses in the lowest economic regions gives the people of these parties the economic stimuli to lessen the conflicts at a micro level, which can then be built upon at the macro level. Although this theory is somewhat untested, there is evidence that this avenue of inquiry has merit, as similar studies within Israel have produced some small successes (Cherry 2014).

Therefore, it is my contention that this avenue of examination applied to a macro level analysis, can offer small yet significant victories in the region, even if it may not solve the issues between these parties. As this is the case, the avenues which I have suggested really have the best chance to be successful in a long term situation, thus attempting to apply them sooner rather than later should be of paramount importance to the international community. Given the lack of concrete successes in the region in regards to peaceful resolutions of long lasting conflicts, even small victories can become paths to probable peaceful solutions. Therefore, any new paths to peace should be considered, lest we see these conflicts continue or escalate.

Various Thoughts

In this volume, I have tried to present work which would spark discussion. It is my intention to share my knowledge with other researchers, with the hopes that they may share like knowledge. It is hope that this will help to spark more discussions in these areas of inquiry, as these are important areas for future cooperative policy creation. In this way, we can hopefully achieve an ongoing conversation amongst the actors involved, which will help in creating a more cooperative international environment. In international relations effective policy creation largely depends on the cooperation of international actors to achieve likeminded goals. The areas of inquiry included in this volume are meant to encourage this type of cooperative dialogue, in order to achieve the likeminded goal of lessening human conflict.

Next issue I will be examining the current position and structural changes involved with Scotland's push towards nationalism, as well as their possible positioning as a European model nation. I hope that you will join us, as we examine the elements which have contributed to this position. Thank you for being a part of this wonderful experiment and we look forward to examining future subjects with you.

Sincerely,

Rev. Dr. Corey T. Oakes, Min.

corey-oakes@hotmail.com

1013 C 5th St.

Wenatchee, Washington

98801

Thesis Bibliography

Al-Ghazali; The Second Discussion; The refutation of their theory of the incorruptibility of the world and of time and motion. Web. Muslim philosophy.com, 8 November 2009. http://www.muslimphilosophy.com/ip/rep/H028.htm

Al-Maturidi, Abu Mansur; The writings of Abu Mansur al-Maturidi on Natural law. The Maturidi School of Sunni Theology. Web. Muslim Philosophy.com,8 November 2009. http://www.muslimphilosophy.com/hmp/16.htm

Augustine, Saint; Confessions, Penguin, London. 1961.Print.

Aquinas, St. Thomas; Summa Theologica I, II. Great Books of the western world, *Encyclopedia Britannica,* 1952, Chicago. Print.

Aristotle; The works of Aristotle II, Nicomachean Ethics, book I; p. 25.

Baltzly, Dirk, "Stoicism", The Stanford Encyclopedia of Philosophy, winter 2012. Edward N. Zalta.ed.Web.Nov. 12 2012. http://plato.stanford.edu/archives/win2012/entries/stoicism/

Benedict, Saint; The rule of Benedict.Web.Nov. 12 2012.< www.osb.org/gen/rule.html.>

Campbell, George; Philosophy of Rhetoric, volume I, p. 114.

Carmichael, Gershom; Natural Rights, and The writings of Gershom Carmichael (1724).

Foriers, Paul and Chaim Perelman, The History of Ideas.

Grotius, Hugo; De iure belli; ac pacis, Prolegomeni XI.

Hobbes, Thomas; Leviathan, chapter XIV.

Jefferson, Thomas and James Madison, The United States Constitution.1786.Web. Nov. 12 2012. www.archives.gov/exhibits/charters/constitution_transcript.html

Religiosity References

"B. Palestinian Pres. Mahmud Abbas, Letter to Israeli PM Benjamin Netanyahu, Ramallah, 14 April 2012."2012. *Journal of Palestine Studies* 41(4):192-194 (https://mywcc.whatcom.edu/OnlineResources/LibraryDatabases.aspx?DirectURL=/docview/1112055782?accountid=2906).

Reuveny, Rafael. 1999. "Israeli-Palestinian Economic Interdependence Reconsidered." *Policy Studies Journal* 27(4):668-671 (https://mywcc.whatcom.edu/OnlineResources/LibraryDatabases.aspx?DirectURL=/docview/210560769?accountid=2906).

<u>Small steps References</u>

Cherry, Robert. "Increased Constructive Engagement Among Israeli Arabs: The Impact of Government Economic Initiatives." Israel Studies, Vol. 19, No. 1 (Spring 2014), pp. 75-97: Indiana University Press. Web. Accessed on: 31 July, 2014. http://www.jstor.org/stable/10.2979/israelstudies.19.1.75.

Oakes, Corey T. "Natural Law as a basis for Inter-religious communications." Esoteric Interfaith Seminary.01 October 2011. Print.

US Department of State: Diplomacy in Action. "Israel 12/28." (1998).Web. Accessed on: 31 July, 2014. http://www.state.gov/outofdate/bgn/israel/5937.htm